Which words or phrases have a similar meaning to the focus word? Write them in the spaces below.

dull

Read 'The Hidden Heart of Me'. Record your thoughts about each of the three questions in the spaces below.

The looking question is ...
How does the narrator behave around other people?

The clue question is ...
How does the narrator feel about herself?

The thinking question is ...
What makes a good friend?

Do you have any questions? Write them here.

Think about the conversations you have had about this text. What more have you learned? Complete the activities below.

Argue that someone who talks all the time might also be insecure.

Discuss the use of the imagery of trapped words in the poem.

Explore ways of making someone feel relaxed around you.

Imagine you are a friend of the narrator and you found out how she had been feeling. What are some things you could do to help her? Write your answer in the thought bubble below.

Feedback

Explore the focus word by completing the activities below.

Write your own definition of the focus word.

Write out the dictionary definition of the focus word.

immigrant

Write down the root part of the word and other variations of the word you can think of.

Make a list of synonyms and antonyms for the focus word.

Draw lines to match the bold word in each sentence to the word or phrase which is closest in meaning. Look up any words you don't know in a dictionary.

The exhausted boxer is **conceding** to his superior opponent.

insufficient resources

There is a **colony** of red ants at the bottom of my garden.

number of people

The children's **independence** in their work, pleased the teacher.

give in

The travellers were surprised at the **poverty** they saw in the remote village.

self guidance

The world's **population** is over seven billion.

a group

Finally, the curious children would **discover** the teacher's age!

treating others badly because of their differences

There is no place for **discrimination** in the world today.

exchange

The excited children all wanted to **trade** football stickers in the playground.

find out

Read 'New York: The Making of a City'. Record your thoughts about each of the three questions in the spaces below.

The looking question is ...
How was Manahatta discovered?

The clue question is ...
Why did people go to live in New York?

The thinking question is ...
What impact did immigration have on New York?

Do you have any questions? Write them here.

Think about the conversations you have had about this text. What more have you learned? Complete the activity below.

Using what you know write a fact file about New York. Remember to use sub-headings and add a feature box to highlight your favourite fact.

Imagine you are interviewing Annie Moore about her emigration to New York City. What questions would you ask? Write three questions on the clipboard below.

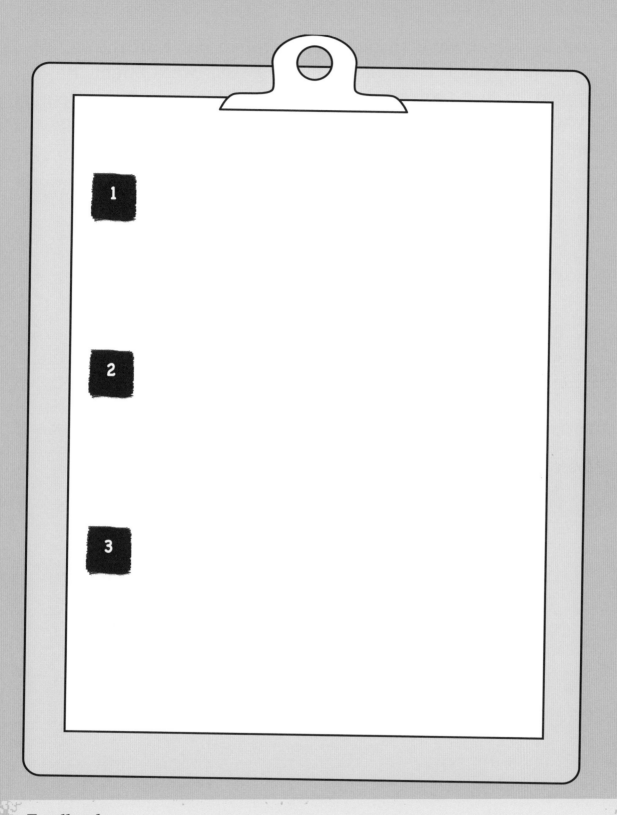

1

2

3

Feedback

Just before he went to bed, Bern popped out with the rubbish. It was a clear night and the stars were bright. He looked up and spotted the Plough, the Hunter and the Dog. Who would have thought that a task as boring as putting out the bins could be so magical!

Find out what the Plough looks like. Draw it here.

Discover why the Hunter constellation is also known as Orion.

Research what the star "the Dog" is also known as.

Explore the focus word by completing the activities below.

What does the focus word mean?

What sort of house has a parlour?

parlour

Write three synonyms for the focus word.

Write a sentence using the focus word.

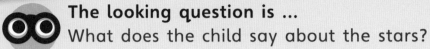

Read the poem 'Escape at Bedtime'. Record your thoughts about each of the three questions in the spaces below.

The looking question is ...
What does the child say about the stars?

The clue question is ...
What happens in the poem?

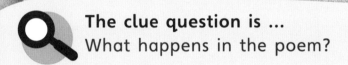

The thinking question is ...
How does the child feel as they look up at the star-filled sky?

Do you have any questions? Write them here.

Think about the conversations you have had about this text. What more have you learned? Complete the activity below.

Describe a time when you have been moved by a sunset, a mountain, a view, the sea or another aspect of nature.

Imagine you are talking to the author of the poem 'Escape at Bedtime'. Write down what you liked about the poem and two things you would change.

I liked ...

I would change ...

I would change ...

Feedback

Do you know what the words below mean? Record your thoughts about each meaning, then look up the words in a dictionary.

I think this word means ...

The definition in the dictionary is ...

survivors

decks

daring

promised

eagerly

Which words or phrases have a similar meaning to the focus word? Write them in the spaces below.

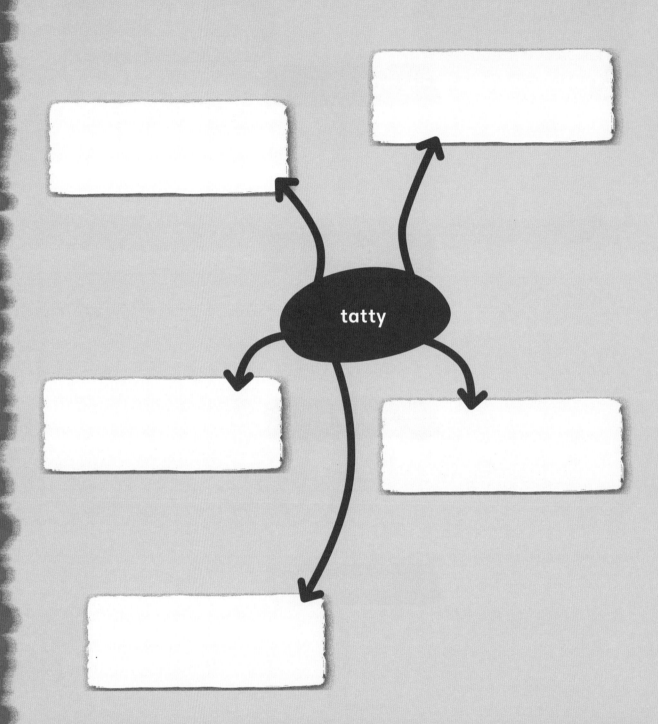

tatty

Read Part 1 of 'Adrift in New York'. Record your thoughts about each of the three questions in the spaces below.

 The looking question is ...
Where is Grace staying and why?

 The clue question is ...
How is Catherine's life different from what Grace is used to?

 The thinking question is ...
Why do you think Grace is so eager for the letter from Auntie Nora to arrive?

Do you have any questions? Write them here.

Think about the conversations you have had about this text. What more have you learned? Complete the activity below.

Describe daily life on Fifth Avenue in New York for Catherine.

How do you think each character will feel about Grace's letter arriving at her aunt's house in Ireland? Write your predictions in the spaces below.

Feedback

Use the bold words to write your own sentences in the spaces provided.

You will always be **welcome** at our house.

Grace left the **mansion** to start her new life with Uncle Patrick.

I've been putting it off ... hoping for a **miracle**.

Can I **borrow** this book?

Can you remember these words from Part 1? Write two sentences using each word in the spaces below.

survivors

promised

eagerly

daring

Adrift in New York • Week 15 • Day 1

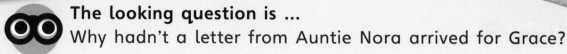

The looking question is ...
Why hadn't a letter from Auntie Nora arrived for Grace?

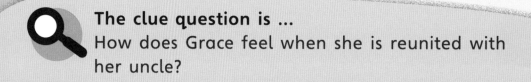

The clue question is ...
How does Grace feel when she is reunited with her uncle?

The thinking question is ...
Do you think Grace and Catherine will remain friends?

Do you have any questions? Write them here.

Think about the conversations you have had about this text. What more have you learned? Complete the activity below.

Explain why Grace and Catherine's friendship is important to each of them.

Summarise what happened in 'Adrift in New York' using the story mountain below.

The problem was ...

Then ...

The problem was solved by ...

In the beginning ...

In the end ...

Feedback

Do you know what the words below mean? Record your thoughts about each meaning, then look up the words in a dictionary.

I think this word means ...

The definition in the dictionary is ...

captive

endangered

smuggled

abandoned

poached

Use the bold words to write your own sentences in the spaces provided.

Giant pandas are in danger of **extinction**.

Parrots are **exotic** birds.

Zoo animals are **confined** to their cages at night.

Selling endangered animals is **illegal** in this country.

Read 'Wild Animals Are Not Pets!'. Record your thoughts about each of the three questions in the spaces below.

The looking question is ...
What are the main reasons wild animals should not be pets?

The clue question is ...
Why do people want wild animals as pets?

? **The thinking question is ...**
Do you think people who own wild animals look after them properly?

Do you have any questions? Write them here.

Think about the conversations you have had about this text. What more have you learned? Complete the activity below.

What would you say to someone who has a tiger as a pet? What questions would you ask them? Write a letter in the space below to one of these people.

What were the consequences of each event in the text?
Write your answers in the spaces below.

The film *Finding Nemo* came out in cinemas.

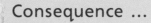
Consequence ...

A cartoon made racoons very popular in Japan.

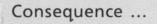
Consequence ...

Feedback

Draw lines to match the bold word in each sentence to the word or phrase which is closest in meaning. Look up any words you don't know in a dictionary.

The bus stopped **abruptly** outside the museum.

deliberately

His watch was his most **valuable** possession.

suddenly and unexpected

The magician **knowingly** mislead the audience.

reduced or faded

The guests to the palace were treated with **honour**.

worth a great deal of money

Regrettably, her mother had to sell her favourite necklace.

unfortunately

The stream had **dwindled** to a trickle by the time I reached the road.

great respect

Read the text and complete the activities below.

The moon's bright belly filled the tiny, barred window. I was trapped in the darkened room, with only the silvery moonlight to see by. Suddenly, the door burst open. My blood ran cold and, fearing for my life, I bolted into the corner of the room as my captors entered.

What does the phrase "the moon's bright belly" tell us about the moon?

What two things are you told about the light in the room?

"I bolted into the corner of the room". What does the word "bolted" tell you about how the person moved?

Read Part 1 of 'Wind Runner and the Hunt'. Record your thoughts about each of the three questions in the spaces below.

The looking question is ...
Which weapons did Wind Runner take with him?

The clue question is ...
Why did Wind Runner fall into the bear trap?

The thinking question is ...
Was Wind Runner right to follow the hunters?

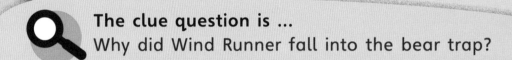

Do you have any questions? Write them here.

Think about the conversations you have had about this text. What more have you learned? Complete the activity below.

How has Wind Runner's confidence changed through the story so far?

What do you think will happen next? Explain your prediction in the space below.

I predict ...

Feedback

Change each word so that it fits in the sentences. Write your answers in the spaces provided.

manoeuvre

The car .... into the parking space.

Despite its size, an oil tanker has great ....

The plane was surprisingly .... and fast for its age.

lone

The moor was a wild and .... place.

My brother likes to spend time by himself – he's a bit of a ....

She suddenly realised that she was all ....

fear

I was .... that I may not make it in time.

He was the most .... of all the brave warriors.

It was as I .... , there was no more cake!

Can you remember these words from Part 1? Write two sentences using each word in the spaces below.

abruptly

honour

regrettably

knowingly

Read Part 2 of 'Wind Runner and the Hunt'. Record your thoughts about each of the three questions in the spaces below.

The looking question is ...
What ways did Wind Runner try to escape the bear?

The clue question is ...
What emotions did Wind Runner experience at the end of the story?

The thinking question is ...
Who was the best hunter in the story?

Do you have any questions? Write them here.

Think about the conversations you have had about this text. What more have you learned? Complete the activity below.

What do you think Wind Runner would do next time he meets a bear?

Circle the words that best describe Wind Runner. Then use your words to write a description of him.

brave   foolhardy   elated   swift   lonely

disobedient   resourceful   resilient   clever

impatient   cowardly   sly   vicious   glum

Feedback

Look up the focus word in a dictionary and write a definition.

Write your own sentence using the focus word.

ancient

Write some synonyms for the focus word.

Write some antonyms for the focus word.

Do you know what the words below mean? Record your thoughts about each meaning, then look up the words in a dictionary.

I think this word means ...

The definition in the dictionary is ...

artefact

malfunctioned

exhibit

redundant

plinth

Read Part 1 of 'The Londorium Transportium'. Record your thoughts about each of the three questions in the spaces below.

The looking question is ...
What is the Transportium?

The clue question is ...
How can you tell this story is set in the future?

? **The thinking question is ...**
Would you like to go to school in the future?

Do you have any questions? Write them here.

The Londorium Transportium • Week 19 • Day 2

Think about the conversations you have had about this text. What more have you learned? Complete the activity below.

What do you think about the author's view of the future? Explain your reasons.

Imagine you are interviewing Nicky B. about the future. What questions would you ask? Write three questions on the clipboard below.

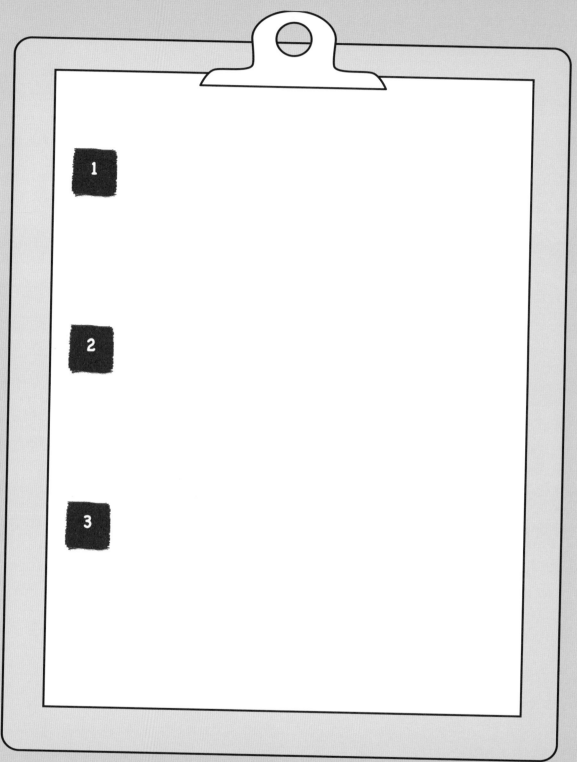

1

2

3

Feedback

Which words or phrases have a similar meaning to the focus word? Write them in the space below.

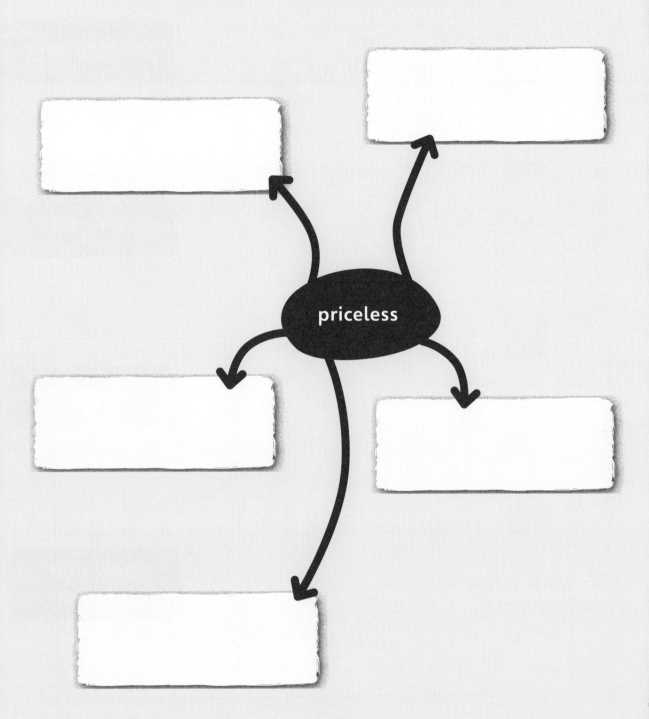

priceless

Woefully, mum swept up the pieces of her broken vase.

looking over

The rabbit **hesitantly** peered out from its burrow.

very old

The town hall provided **sanctuary** for the earthquake victims.

sadly

An **ancient** pyramid stood before them.

slow and unsure

As the teachers entered the room they stopped, **surveying** the class before them.

a safe place

Read Part 2 of 'The Londorium Transportium'. Record your thoughts about each of the three questions in the spaces below.

The looking question is ...
How did the artefacts end up on the floor?

The clue question is ...
How did Mr Hodgson feel during this part of the story?

The thinking question is ...
Do you think the children enjoyed the school trip?

Do you have any questions? Write them here.

Think about the conversations you have had about this text. What more have you learned? Complete the activity below.

Imagine you are Mr Hodgson writing a letter to apologise to the Transportium. Write the letter below.

Summarise what happened in 'The Londorium Transportium' using the story mountain below.

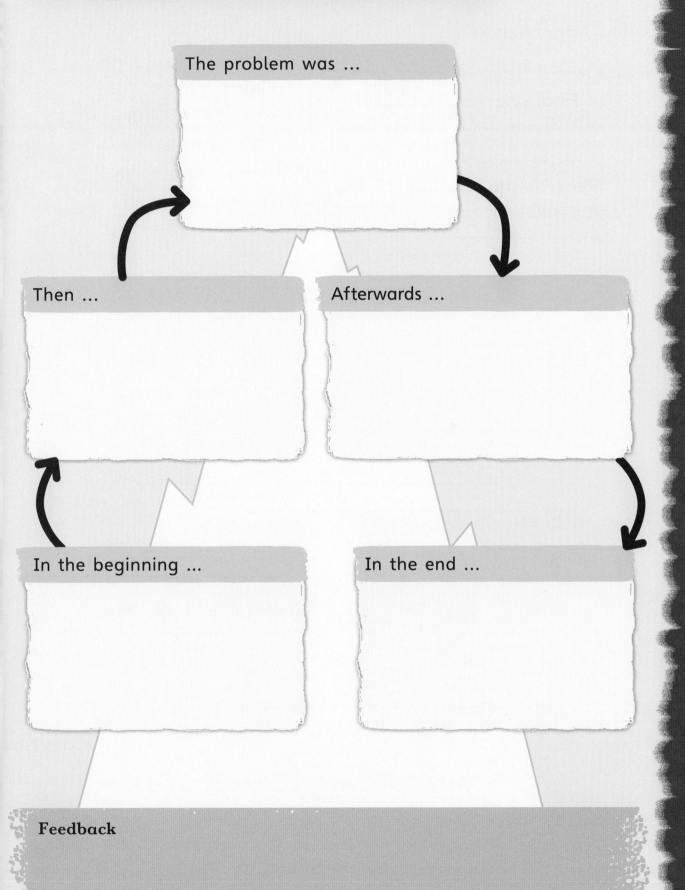

The problem was ...

Then ...

Afterwards ...

In the beginning ...

In the end ...

Feedback

Reading Goals

This term I aim to …

Find a new author I like!

Read a play with friends!

Read the book of my favourite film!

Learn a poem by heart!

Group Discussion Rules

- We will listen carefully to the person who is speaking

- Everyone should have a chance to speak

- We will give reasons for our ideas

- We can ask others for reasons if they don't say them

- **We can agree and disagree politely with each other**

- We will respect each other's ideas and opinions

- We will share all the information in the group

- We will try to reach an agreement together if we can

Add any other group discussion rules your class or group has decided on here:

- ....

- ....

- ....

- ....

- ....

Reading Tracker

Book title: ....

Author: ....

Date finished: .... Score out of 10 ☐

Book title: ....

Author: ....

Date finished: .... Score out of 10 ☐

Book title: ....

Author: ....

Date finished: .... Score out of 10 ☐

Book title: ....

Author: ....

Date finished: .... Score out of 10 ☐

Book title: ....

Author: ....

Date finished: .... Score out of 10 ☐

Book title: ....

Author: ....

Date finished: .... Score out of 10 ☐

Book title: ....

Author: ....

Date finished: .... Score out of 10 ☐

Book title: ....

Author: ....

Date finished: .... Score out of 10 ☐

Book title: ....

Author: ....

Date finished: .... Score out of 10 ☐

Book title: ....

Author: ....

Date finished: .... Score out of 10 ☐

Read-alikes

If you liked 'Hidden Heart of Me', why not try ...

A is Amazing! Poems About Feelings
by Wendy Cooling

If you liked 'New York: The Making of a City', why not try ...

Not For Parents New York
by Klay Lamprell

We Are All Born Free
by Amnesty International

If you liked 'Escape at Bedtime', why not try ...

National Geographic Book of Nature Poetry
by J Patrick Lewis

If you liked 'Adrift in New York', why not try ...

Tom's Midnight Garden Graphic Novel
by Philippa Pearce

Rooftoppers
by Katherine Rundell

If you liked 'Wild Animals Are Not Pets!', why not try ...

Bizarre Beasts by Steve Backshall

The Curiositree: Natural World by AJ Wood and Mike Jolley

If you liked 'Wind Runner and the Hunt', why not try ...

Apache
by Tanya Landman

Trickster: Native American Tales
by Matt Dembicki

If you liked 'The Londorium Transportium', why not try ...

Time Travelling with a Hamster
by Ross Welford

Day of the Assassins
by Johnny O'Brien

Tick the types of text you have read this term!

Funny story ☐

MYTH ☐

GRAPHIC NOVEL ☐

FANTASY STORY ☐

JOKE book ☐

Scary story ☐

Story set in another country ☐

Story set a long time ago ☐

Newspaper article ☐

Poetry book ☐

Book of facts ☐

Magazine ☐

Fairy tale ☐

Play script ☐

Science fiction story ☐

Picture book ☐

Comic ☐

SOMETHING ELSE? WRITE IT HERE:

The best new words I have learned this term

Word	What it means
conceding	accepting that something is going to happen whether you like it or not

The best jokes I have read this term

Where do cows go on holiday?

Moo York!

Reading Record

Fill in these sheets for one story you have chosen yourself.

At the beginning

Title:

Author:

Why did you choose this book?

What score do you think you'll give it? /10

Who is the character you like most?

Has anything like this ever happened to you?

What questions do you have about the story?

What do you think will happen at the end?

At the end

Were your predictions right?

Is there anything that still puzzles you?

What score would you give this book? | /10 |

Who do you think would enjoy this book?

The best facts I have read this term

Best Fact

New York used to be called New Amsterdam.

Best Fact

Best Fact

Best Fact

Best Fact

Recommended Reads for Me

Think about someone in your group, class or family. What books would you recommend for them?

Recommended Reads for

A story I think they'll like:

A non-fiction book I think they'll like:

A poem I think they'll like:

An author I think they'll like:

What books have been recommended for you? Write them here.

Bug Club Comprehension is a fresh new approach that helps every child master comprehension. It uses a powerful and proven talk-based, mastery approach to help children develop a deeper understanding of texts.

Part of the Bug Club Comprehension programme, the workbooks provide:

- activities for each day of the teaching cycle
- clear, child-friendly designs that complement the accompanying texts
- formative assessment opportunities
- a 'Reading Journal' section for children to record their independent reading.

Series Consultants:
Wayne Tennent and David Reedy
Workbook and Teaching Card Authors:
Catherine Casey, Sarah Snashall and Andy Taylor

Published by Pearson Education Limited, 80 Strand, London, WC2R 0RL.

www.pearsonschools.co.uk

Text © Pearson Education Limited 2017

Designed by Bigtop Design Ltd
Original illustrations © Pearson Education Limited 2017
Illustrated by Olga Demidova, Shahab Shamshirsaz, Kevin Hopgood, Alan Marks and Amit Tayal

First published 2017

24

17

British Library Cataloguing in Publication Data
A catalogue record for this book is available from the British Library

ISBN 978 0 435 18592 3

Printed in the UK by Bell and Bain Ltd.

Acknowledgements
The publisher would like to thank the following for their kind permission to reproduce their photographs in this workbook and accompanying photocopiable activities:

Alamy Images: Tierfotoagentur 31b, PCM_11b, PCM_12c; **Fotolia.com**: Gianfranco Bella 30, Piotr Szczap 31, PCM_11t, PCM_12t; **Shutterstock.com**: Robbi 57, 62, Songquan Deng 10, warmer PCM_12b

Cover images: Front: **Fotolia.com**: Piotr Szczap

All other images © Pearson Education